How a curator's wanderlust helps us to unlock the door to a broader worldview, offering differing perspectives of everyday 'things'.

Written by Matthew Jan Bilski
Design and Photography by Yu-mei Huang
Curated by Jill Tsai

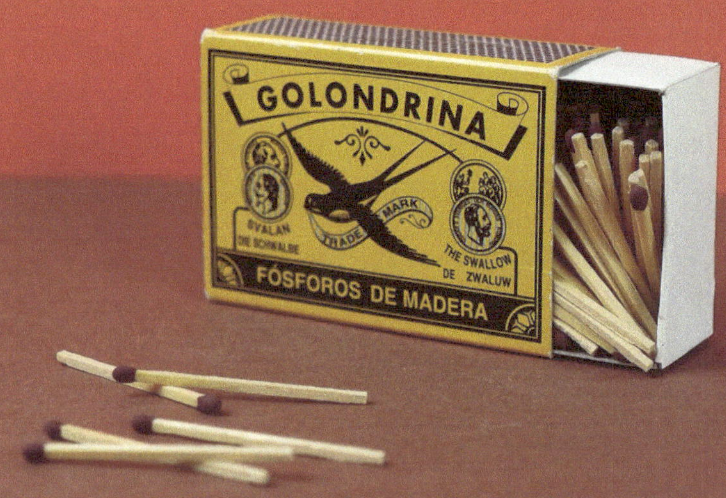

Above: *FÓSFOROS DE MADERA "LA GOLONDRINA" from Madrid, Spain. 2018*

Contents

Introduction

This is a book about connected beliefs, curated through the keen eye of a world traveller with an artistic vision for how similar-looking objects have different meanings according to their setting and usage. These objects help us to gain new perspectives on the everyday, but also build our understanding of the world.

This book invites you to approach these objects with an open mind, and find potential different meanings, connectivity or symbolism behind them. This book therefore is not written from an expert's perspective, but as a manifestation of the curator's personal passion for world artefacts - objects that we still have a lot to learn from.

Above: Chocolate milk drink called Matilde, popular amongst children and known everywhere in Denmark, Paradiso Grønne Peberkorn, lobster paste, 'Medova' Tea, a tube (more popular than bottles or jars) of mayonnaise, books on architecture and porcelain, and a bottle of French Bearnaise sauce from Copenhagen, Denmark. 2018

Here at Travel Things, we appreciate that one's perspectives are very subjective and personal, and so we would be keen to hear your thoughts too, which we accept could differ from ours.

Take for example this selection of everyday items from Copenhagen, which demonstrate the approach to curation taken in this book. Here is a variety of 'things' presented in a neat composition of pastel colours, which to the curator mapped the architectural landscape or natural environment in which these items are used. Such an approach helps us to shape fond memories of a place, share our feelings and impressions of it, and build our overall understanding of it.

The selection in this book draws examples from Travel Things' wider collection – some with more obvious meanings, such as watering cans and brooms, through to what might feel less immediately obvious to us, such as lottery receipts or camel muzzles. It teaches us about the different use of materials, applying varied solutions to everyday problems, from the culinary, to the agricultural or sartorial. We can learn lessons from some of these examples in our own lives. For example using sustainable and traditional materials in place of our more modern consumer goods that create waste and cause a negative environmental impact. We look also at traditional practices for controlling animals, and explore how our religious or political beliefs are represented in the objects we encounter on our travels. Finally, we see how natural mementos , such as leaves and seed pods, can evoke the tactile richness of travel, helping to shape our memories.

Travel Things therefore is not here to give all the answers on the objects presented in its collection, but is a more playful and creative approach, asking us questions about various cultures and places, valuing their similarities as well as differences. It is intended to help us question why we travel and what we take from these journeys, through the things we encounter along the way. This book invites you to think about the everyday objects you discover on your trips abroad, and what they teach you about that place and your own world perspectives. Our intention, therefore, is to inspire you to embrace the world in your future travels. We do not always have the definitive take on these objects, but we take joy in their exploration.

Artisanal passions: from the Mediterranean to the Pacific

This page is all about artisanal passions, set across two countries. It invites us to ask how these objects are used every day – all objects depicted here are handmade, on-site (amongst various similar everyday items), all the more impressive when we consider how cheaply mass-produced equivalents can be purchased from large retailers. On the one hand, a bucket, and whistles from Pizzo, Italy, made by the same craftsman, and the other, a watering can from Tainan, Taiwan's oldest city, and cultural capital, famed for its rich culture, street food and traditional cuisine.

They each symbolise one's life as a passion for creating beautiful objects, as a connectivity of love for their trade. It shows us something human that sits below culture or geography, how behind similar materials and universally recognisable objects we are not all that different, despite the strong cultural associations one makes with both countries - think Italy, with its cuisine, Mediterranean flair, ancient history, and Taiwan - the beautiful isle with its traditions, ocean views, tropical forests and mountains. And yet, here we see none of that influence but a distillation of a more fundamental passion for creating everyday and practical items, to an exceptional quality, as a thing of artisanal beauty.

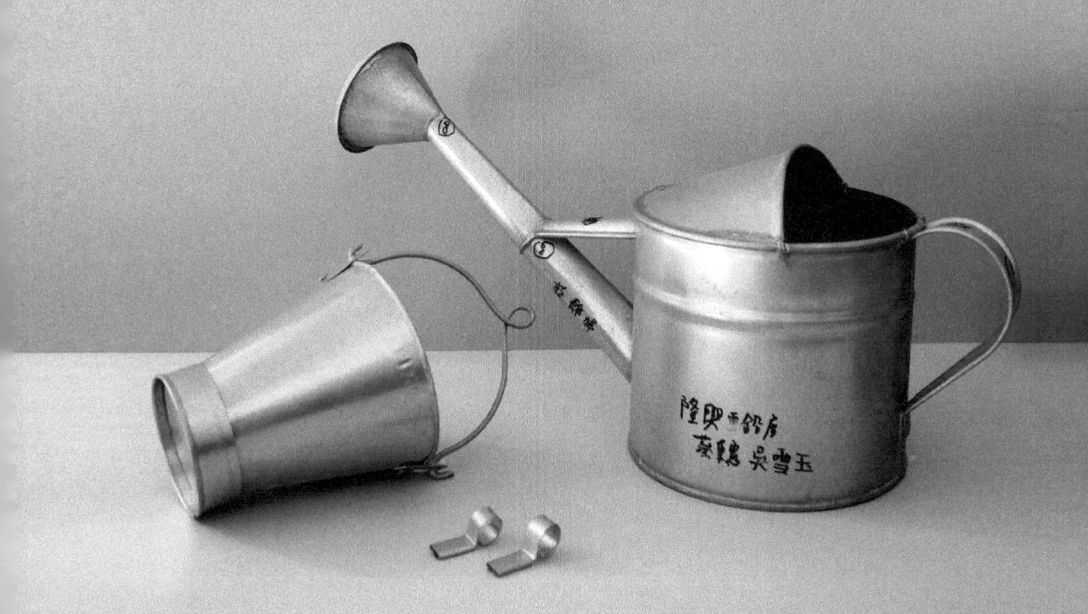

New materials, same old form...

All items here originate from Palau, Micronesia - two types of taro peeler, one made from giant clam, the other a more modern stainless steel, and separately a hoe, or digging tool, whose head is also sculpted traditionally from a giant clam, with a wooden handle, used as an agricultural or garden tool. This presents the pragmatism of adapting to a modern reality - that of giant clams becoming a vulnerable marine life, with populations diminishing quickly. The giant clam has become extinct in many areas, and conservationists are concerned about its overexploitation. All the while, we have a more sustainable stainless steel equivalent, where the traditional aesthetic and functionality endures.

This alteration in source materials preserves a beautiful hand-crafting tradition. It otherwise needs no further fix, despite the presence of modern and cheap mass-produced tools – as they say, if it ain't broke...

Disposable or reusable?

The items depicted opposite contrast natural and sustainable materials with a more manufactured approach, both rooted in deep tradition. Here we have cutlery sets - one of Jamaican calabash, the other Korean stainless steel (Sujeo set). On the latter, legend has it that Korean metal chopsticks originate from the Baekje era (18 B.C.- 660 A.D.), a period in which the royal family used silver chopsticks, which were thought to become discoloured upon contact with poison in their food. In time the practice became widespread, with more affordable stainless steel. Jamaican kitchenware similarly follows a deep-rooted tradition, from biodegradable calabash, used as a utensil, container, or musical instrument. This set consists of a colander, utensils and bowls, typically used across the West Indies. Calabash is considered consistent with the practice of Ital living; of using only natural products, and traditional equipment for recipes passed down through generations.

This is therefore a narrative of disposable versus reusable utensils, where both are eco-friendly, and developed from differing longstanding traditions, still used widely in the modern era. We invite you to consider which style you prefer for your daily needs.

Form can be deceiving

These objects tell a story of similar-looking triangular items playing very different roles – a tale of shape versus function. First, two cone-shaped containers called Sri Lankan steamer, or 'Neethupeddi', used to boil or steam Pittu (coconut rice, savoury or sweet). These items (top and middle) are hand-made from large palmyrah leaves of Jaffna, Sri Lanka. The third (below) object is an exfoliating back-scrub from Aqaba, Jordan, made from palm fibres – a traditional bathroom accessory.

All three items show us how something similar-looking can have a very different meaning across different cultures. They lead us to ask, from a product design point of view, why is a familiar shape important? Why should a triangle be more effective than, say, a disc- or square-shaped steamer or back scrub? What other triangular items do you use day-to-day? Pyramid teabags, perhaps?

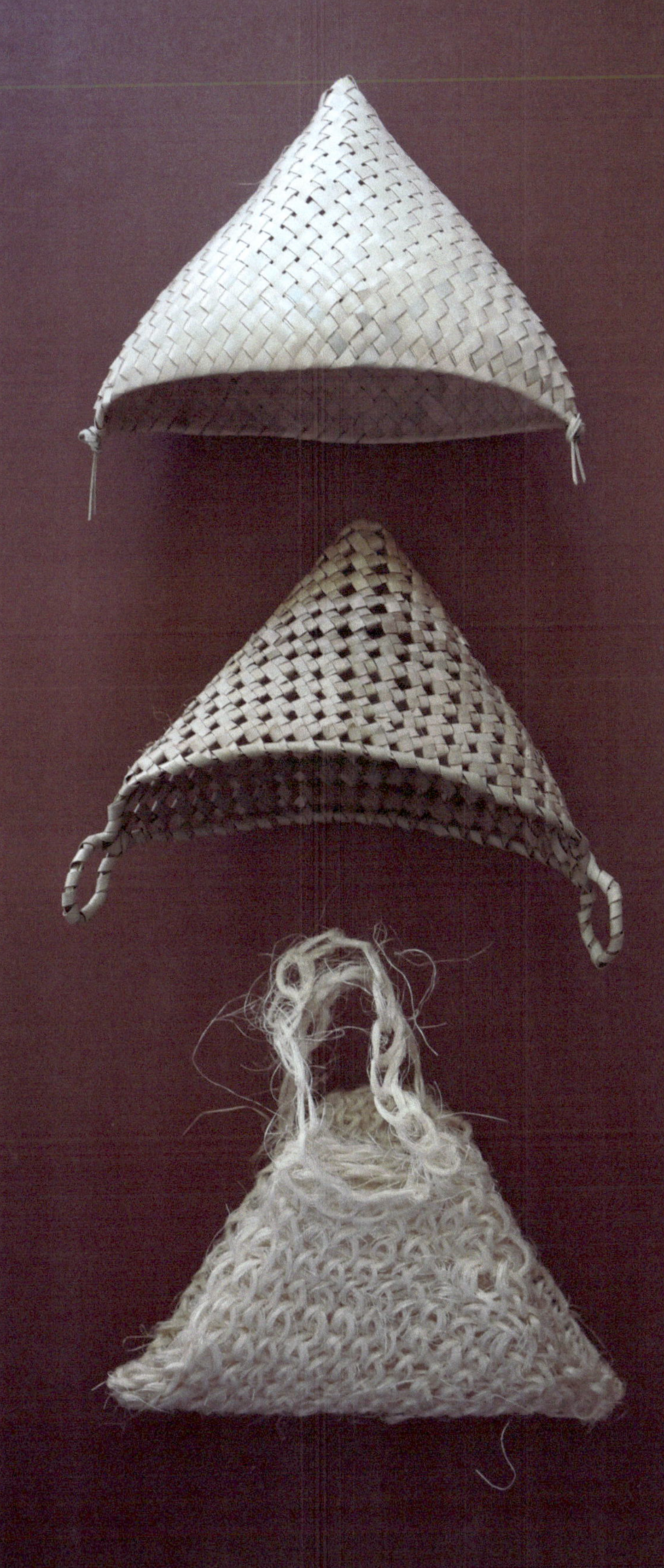

Bowled over

These items hail from a similar region, and tell the story of how a simple everyday object like a bowl can have different meanings across cultures. This includes, to the left, a typical Taiwanese steamed rice pudding bowl, commonly known as 'Whay Guay'. This is used to contain liquidised rice, mixed with different savoury flavours, for example shiitake (or various types of) mushrooms and dried shallots, steamed to form a firm sticky, but savoury pudding-like texture. It is usually served with ground garlic, sweet soy sauce and on rare occasion even wasabi. Another bowl is placed upturned over the top to keep the flies off in the hot and humid summer. On the right, a Hong Kong 'beer bowl,' or 'fighting bowl' (written on the outer rim of the bowl) used in drinking contests held in open-air food stalls (known as 'Dai pai dong'). On downing a bowlful (or shot) of beer, the contestant triumphantly slams the vessel down on the table to show, on the floor of the bowl, the character for 'victory'.

Here we have two examples of ordinary bowls used in different ways, for very different reasons, teaching us about versatility, and how an object as simple as a bowl has a lot more than meets the eye.

勝

See-through

Here we find Capiz shells from Vigan, a Spanish colonial town in the Philippines. They are used as so-called 'windowpane oysters', slotted into a grid-pattern window frame as panes of translucent. They look like white flattened pearls, which glow in the sunshine. Below is a bronze Spanish peephole, or 'Mirilla'. These peepholes are historically found in traditional doors of larger Spanish buildings, such as castles and mansions, about the size of one's head. They include a novel opening mechanism consisting of two pieces, respectively on the inner then outer sides of a door. The inner piece has a handle to open or close the 'eyelashes'. This piece is from Madrid, again connected with Spanish colonialism. They are therefore much larger than the tiny peepholes we are more familiar with on modern doors, and are used as a form of defence, for example for firing arrows through. We wonder what else might these have been used for – ventilation during the summer heat, or just seeing what is going on outside? Both items serve the purpose of looking through, one more opaquely, the other more covertly, and teach us about different architectural approaches in each country, across time. It begs the question, what is see-through and what is not?

Beauty on the beast

The items directly above are Omani camel muzzles: a more modern twist on a centuries-old design, and part of a current trend to craft from a mixture of bright, multicoloured cotton and plastic. These muzzles are used to prevent the camels from scavenging or spitting. Above right are cockerel leg straps, used widely in cock fighting, or 'sabong', in the Philippines. These brightly coloured straps are from Siargao Island, but a variety of different types are used nationwide, similarly brightly coloured.

The theme here is how humans, for different purposes, control animals through use of objects that are, equally colourful, following similar artistic styles and use of traditional or modern materials. Every society has its own version of everyday tethers, leashes or fetters to control animals. Do we subconsciously embellish these objects with bright, cheerful colours to cheer up the affected animals, or perhaps to mask our guilt in curtailing their freedom?

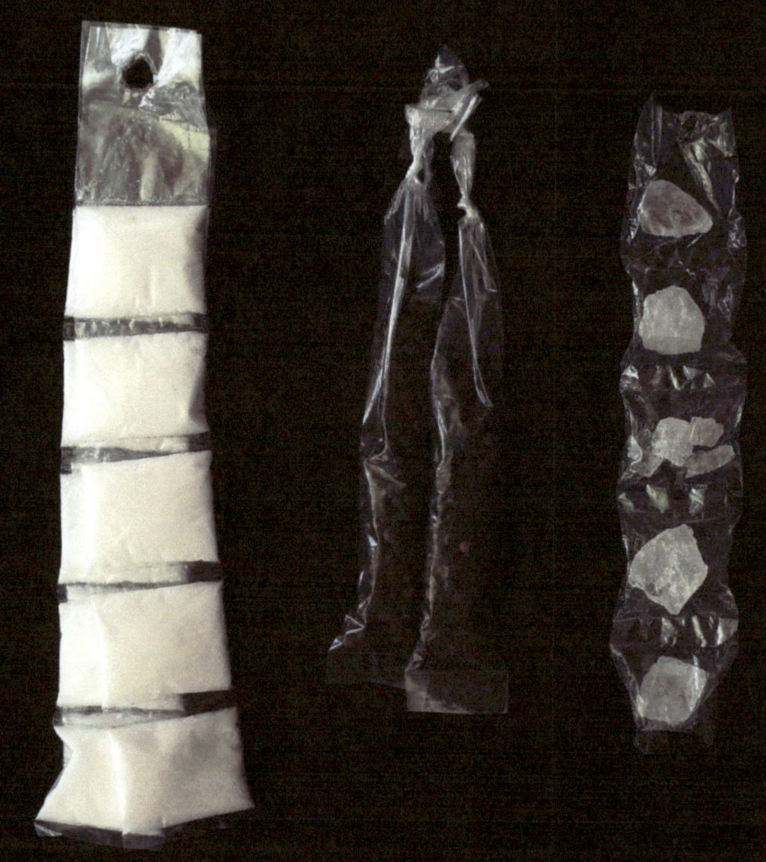

Is less really more?

This is about an economic fix creating environmental issues. Within Philippine's 'sachet-economy', across many of its small islands, sachets are popular because of their affordability, convenience and durable packaging. Small quantities of every-day products are sold in communities nationwide. However, plastic waste from these sachets is expensive to manage, difficult to recycle, and cannot be reused, which is very problematic in local communities. This is a unique and innovative example of buying small,

which also helps reduce waste from unused products, instead of the bulk buying we might be more familiar with in our supermarkets. However, we still pay a price for this convenience, as is the case the world over, whether buying big or small, through the impact of our waste on our local environment. It prompts us to ask what's the right way to reduce waste – should we buy large and so reduce packaging, or buy little to waste less unused produce?

Life is a lottery

Taiwan has in place an innovative 'Receipt Lottery', in operation since the 1950s. Issued by merchants in their routine business, receipts are kept by both seller and consumer, each with an eight-digit number, for taxation proposes, managed by the government. It exists in many forms such as hand-written, printed copies, and more recently digital form. A lottery is drawn every two months, with various cash prizes, up to $10 million NT (New Taiwan dollars). The government devised the Receipt Lottery to encourage accountancy best-practice and ensure higher VAT receipts. With the prospect of winning potential millions, customers demand receipts with every purchase and merchants record all their transactions properly.

This shows us how something so ordinary and mundane as a receipt (at least to us non-accountants from outside of Taiwan), can generate a lot of excitement amongst locals and create a win-win-win situation (for consumers, with potential winnings, retailers through better accountancy, and government through more tax revenue). Perhaps one we should suggest to Her Majesty's Revenue and Customs here in the UK?

電子發票證明聯
108年09-10月
UZ-87298907
2019-10-04 17:36:01
隨機碼:4867
總計:200

Porcelain pleasures, plastic free

Here is a unique everyday health product – a popular local speciality known as an 'old-Beijing yogurt' (Nai Lao), served in charactersitic pure white porcelain containers. The yogurt is prepared by heating milk and adding sugar. Its name comes from its unique and traditional method of yogurt making, typically in three varieties – original, low fat and honey, more than one of which may include the addition of nuts, raisins and rice wine.

What is unusual in a modern consumer-driven city like Beijing is that each pot must be returned to the vendor after use (who kindly made an exception for the Travel Things Museum). Although nowadays some yogurts are sold in plastic containers too, we see here a more traditional porcelain approach - an example avoiding unnecessary waste packaging with exquisite reusable materials, that only add to the popularity of this product.

Healing dolls

This page deals with religious artefacts. These paper dolls, known as Hitogata or Katashiro, are used as part of a purification ritual at Shinto shrines in Japan, where one transfers their impure energy, sins, or misfortune into the dolls through writing down their name and age, rubbing the doll on one's body and breathing on it. A voluntary contribution, typically between 200 to 3,000 yen, is placed in an envelope and offered to the spirits. Different shrines have differing approaches to this custom. Similarly, we see here a Taiwanese 'spirit carrier' figure made of straw or paper, both male and female, and also figures representing the 12 signs of the Chinese zodiac. The difference between them lies in the extent of intricate detail in the Taiwanese straw version, compared to the more austere Japanese white paper dolls. Both are part of rituals that help us stay peaceful, aimed at cleansing oneself of negative thoughts, whether a broken heart, lack of energy or fixating on past experiences. We see here similar customs across two geographies, both of which are examples of a phenomenon that, like religious prayer, modern psychology would seek to explain as part of a mental healing process, and problem solving for repressed emotions. What emotions would you want to transfer to a paper doll?

Faith in travel

We have here a Bulgarian Orthodox triptych, used in households as a focus for prayer. Alongside this sits a baby Jesus from the Philippines, also used in family homes and showing the Spanish colonial influence with a local flavour to it,. The third item is a Taiwanese Taoist figurine called 'Tudigong', a Taoist goddess of land and wealth. Finally, a pocket-sized bible from Barcelona, no larger than a smartphone and perfect for travellers. Also, a coconut coil from Sri Lanka, from a Buddhist temple, which a priest will tie around your wrist for protection, as long as you pay for it.

These are all objects that act as a focus of worship across several religions and continents, showing us how varied religious practices and belief systems manifest themselves differently, and provide comfort - whether for personal protection, prosperity, faith or tackling existential quandary.

Common Communists

With a focus here on political beliefs, this page depicts Communist thought leaders across China, Cuba and Bulgaria, the latter consisting of a recording of one of Lenin's speeches in 1916, in the build-up to Russia's Communist revolution. This presents the idea of connected beliefs across continents and very disparate cultures, where Communism ultimately came to take root.

These objects exemplify a tendency of a significant number of people to shape political standpoints through a hagiographic fixation on the figureheads of a particular ideology, in this case various Communist leaders, revered (or reviled) by fellow countrymen in their rise to power. We see a theme here across this and the previous two chapters, on belief, faith, objects of worship and iconography.

Д-16693-4

В. И. ЛЕНИН

V. I. LENIN

Speeches recorded

in 1919 and 1920

Natural travel mementos (a curator's quirk...)

This page shows us how mementos gifted by nature conjure up treasured memories of our travels, through aromatic, visual and tactile form. This museum's curator has a quirky habit of stashing such objects in her pockets or suitcase, as a personal reminder of the places she has travelled to, like a postcard, travel journal or tacky souvenir. These objects are wrapped in her feeling of particular places, from soft seeds floating on the wind in Barcelona, crisp leaves from outside Monaco's Monte Carlo casino, cotton grass from Iceland, driven on a bitter cold summer wind across a lunar-like landscape, to a ground littered by gold-yellow Cape Verde seed pods from Mindelo, or mahogany seed pods from the streets of Barbados.

Each of these items capture the raw power of natural surroundings to evoke memories of our travels as much as memories of the people, culture and built environment. These natural elements give us a sense of time (the passing seasons), and romance. They serve as a further means of logging our journeys besides travel journals, photos and personal anecdotes. Most of us surely have our own quirks for reminding ourselves of our travels – from train or bus tickets, city maps or even purloined beermats... what are yours?

Sweet money

Here we have Euro sugar money, in the form of sweet edible paper (aka rice paper) from Barcelona, Spain, and various types of sugar sachet from Sofia, Bulgaria. These are examples of an imaginative approach to portraying common currency in everyday confectionary or packaging, bringing a creative spark to something as mundane as money.

To the traveller, the feel, sight and usage of new banknotes in different countries is part of the excitement of our journeys; its artistic representation here helps to evoke that element of joy (and sweeten the deal for travel expenditure).

Come wind, rain or shine

The theme here is protection from the natural environment, and how the exigencies of weather and climate can create objects of true beauty across cultures. Firstly, a 'Vakul', or a rain cape, worn by the Ivatan women on Batanes island, Philippines. Then, a hand-woven coconut-leaf fan from Thailand. Similarly, we have a Burmese Kyauk Pyin stone slab, and Thanaka log, whose bark is ground down into a paste and used as a secret beauty treatment by Burmese women, and as natural sun protection, useful if you forget your sunscreen. Finally, to Lesotho, the so-called 'kingdom in the sky', and its iconic headwear, or 'mokorotlo', a traditional straw hat. This is a national symbol, featured on the Lesotho flag, inspired by the conical Mount Qiloane. The hat is particularly useful for herders in such a windy country with high night to daytime extremes of warm and cold temperatures.

These items show us how across four continents, over the centuries people have developed traditional approaches towards combatting the elements and building comfort for themselves in adapting to their local environment. As Brits who love to talk about the weather, here are some good conversation starters for your travels! (Perhaps we should also consider umbrellas as part of our national symbolism?)

Tobacco travels well

The theme here is tobacco, and different means of ingesting the leaves of these controversial plants worldwide. They range from single-purchase Filipino cigarettes in a jar, to a Taiwanese cigarette tub, whether ironically or ignorantly, branded as promoting 'Long Life'. We also see here 'wet' (pre-cured) tobacco leaf rolls from Cape Verde, which tradition dictates can only be sold by men (but we do not know why this is the case!). The different ways to consume tobacco seem endless, from Swedish youths taking snus on a night out, to the more intricate ritual of a hookah and shisha, from Jordan.

From its origins in pre-Columbian America, to its later introduction to Europe and the rest of the world, despite

our modern understanding of its harmful effects on our health, the range of rituals and habits associated with tobacco consumption show us how for centuries it has endured across so many cultures. Despite scientific consensus on its damaging effects, tobacco is a common means of social cohesion that continues to draw people together throughout the globe.

1. " Reyna Mascadas" (from Spanish colonial times)
2. 501 cigarettes from St Lucia (but made in India)
3. A tub of Taiwanese "Long Life" cigarettes
4. A jar of individual-sale cigarettes; one cigarette costs 3 peso
5. Jamaican coconut chalice
6. Hookah and shisha set from Aqaba, Jordan
7. Bambu rolling paper
8. Chinese brass pipe from Beijing
9. Homemade pipes from Cape Verde
10. Waxy paper packed into teardrop shaped cigarettes from Barbados (you can find locals selling them on every public beach)
11. Swedish snus from Stockholm
12. M. Rastafari chillum pipe from Gibraltar
13. Wet raw tobacco leaf roll from Cape Verde

6

13

11

12

Better neutral and natural

Here we have a selection of eco-friendly natural tools and materials, showing how we can be more sustainable by avoiding plastics, and return to traditional practices. These objects vary from Taiwanese graters and lunch boxes to seemingly more niche objects such as utensils for making dumplings or a lice picker (comb) from Sri Lanka – a

smart approach to an uncommon problem we might face wherever we travel! These objects, with their understated tones, show us that in face of environmental challenges and the limitations of our throw-away consumerism of gaudy plastics, the old ways are often best; something we can learn from wherever we travel.

Cleanliness begins at home

Here we focus on the timeless matter of household cleaning, with a selection of brooms and brushes from Oman, St Lucia, Spain and Bulgaria. These objects show us how the act of maintaining cleanliness and removing dust and debris from our floors is universal, and our approach to this problem varies little across countries and time. As well as seeking out what makes us different, sometimes it is good to celebrate our similarities in the less exotic elements of our lives.

1. *Omani date fruit stalks used as a broom*
2. *St Lucia latanye leaf brush*
3. *Spanish esparto grass hand-brush*
4. *Bulgaria broom handcrafted from hay*

The mundane and usual can bring us a sense of familiarity and feeling of home comfort when travelling, whether something as simple as a commonplace dustpan and brush, or a more elaborate broom. Our museum curator assures us that these brushes have unique and distinct smells, from the rich aroma of Omani date trees, to the smell of latanye leaves (she has a funny habit of sniffing brooms!).

Unlocking our curiosity

Finally, we return full circle to Denmark, to a puzzling travel discovery – a collection of keyholes seen on the walls of buildings in the old town of Copenhagen. Not immediately obvious to the uninitiated traveller, we cannot help asking what are these locks for? Perhaps purely decorative, a memento from former residents, or a partner who has moved out, symbolising the unravelling of relationships, or leaving your key in a key cemetery! Or perhaps they are purely functional – a lock to a key deposit tube, useful for deliveries, building maintenance or the fire brigade. But in that case, how do we know which keys belong to which doors? And what are we opening by unlocking a wall? The true meaning of these keys might be obvious to Danish residents, but it is more fun to end this book with an open-ended question.

This is a fitting conclusion to a book designed to promote our inquisitive minds and natural curiosity when it comes to travel, and seeing things as an outsider – an uninformed traveller. It is our questioning of these 'travel things' that help us to understand, to learn and see the world through different eyes, helping to bring us all a little bit closer. Finding answers to our questions when travelling, or even just asking the question in the first place, helps us to unlock the door to an expansive and more coherent world view.

With thanks to

Matthew Jan Bilski

Matthew Bilski lives in west London. He has previously travelled the world, or bits of it, and lived in Japan for several years. His hobbies include playing music, especially piano, writing and running, whenever he finds the time. Most of his free time these days is taken up by fatherhood, and spending time with his family, as proud father of two boys. Originally from the north of England – Cheshire, to be precise, he has lived in and around London for just over a decade. He aspires to one day continue his world adventures, to further explore the places and things described in this book and beyond.

Yu-mei Huang

Yu mei Huang is a Taiwanese-born, London-based craft maker. Having graduated from the Royal College of Art Masters programme, she focuses on textile manipulation. Her work is characterised by vibrant colours and three-dimensional textures. Besides textiles and fashion, she also works freelance on image creation and graphic design. Knitting Industry Creative has described her work as "Bold and Funky Sculpture". She combines innovative processes, valuing craftsmanship and allowing different materials to shape her practice. Her work pushes the boundaries between body and space. However, her aesthetic plays an important role in this publication from photoshoot and set design, woven into graphic design. You can find out more about her on www.yumei-Huang.com or her Instagram @yumeihuang_studio.

travel
things

Published in 2021 by Jill HC Tsai (UK) for Travel Things Museum London (travelthingsmuseum.com)

Written by Matthew Jan Bilski

Edited by Elinor K C Hatt

Design and Photography by Yu-mei Huang

Curated by Jill Tsai

Cover Design: Travel Things Museum

A catalogue record for this book is available from the British Library.

ISBN : 978-0-9575772-4-4

This 52 pages colour paperback book is available through the Amazon store in the United Kingdom, printed and bound by Kindle Direct Publishing.

www.ingramcontent.com/pod-product-compliance
Lightning Source LLC
LaVergne TN
LVHW052310100826
845147LV00006B/719

* 9 7 8 0 9 5 7 5 7 7 2 4 4 *